KULLEH GRASI

# TELL ME,
# KENYALANG

KULLEH GRASI

# TELL ME, KENYALANG

*translated from*

*Malay by*

PAULINE FAN

ISBN 978-1-949918-01-4

**Published by:**
Circumference Books
85 East End Avenue #14F
New York, New York 10028
*www.circumferencebooks.com*

**Distributed by:**
Small Press Distribution (SPD)
1341 Seventh Street
Berkeley, California 94710-1409
*www.spdbooks.org*

Printed by KOPA® *www.kopa.eu.*

**Acknowledgements**

I give thanks:
To the Petara, the gods who begin each mosaic.
To Apak, Mak, Lenny, and Sherry, who offered the space and foundations of
my creative life.
To my beloved comrades, Nading Rhapsody—the narratives I inscribe for you
are flower pollen that we harvest through the seasons of this journey.
To Raygyna Hayden—thank you for being my eyes and ears on this odyssey.
Alvina Thomas, Elvina Bong, Kak Ain, Florence Lasam, Opah Aspa, the
women who have shaped the path of my emotional being.
Pauline Fan—this journey together has been utterly beautiful!
Special thanks to Jennifer Kronovet and Dan Visel of Circumference Books.
And you,
Christ Sheldon, Tommy Ding, Aidan Assahari. Without all of you, I am a
worn-out atlas. Let this tale become history.

I, Kulleh Grasi.

# Contents

**Kulleh Grasi's
Entangled Universe**
*Pauline Fan*

THE WORLD KULLEH GRASI EVOKES IN HIS POETRY is both present and absent—it is seen and longed for, remembered and forgotten. It is the real and reimagined world of the poet's homeland, Sarawak, the Malaysian state that stretches along the northwest coast of Borneo. Grasi's Sarawak is a place where all things are "narrated, alive"—where Iban *ensera* tales, the call of omen birds, the drone of primetime news, and the roar of bulldozers coexist in perpetual oscillation between polyphony and dissonance. Here, the poet listens to the language of rivers and stones, to the leopard's footsteps, and the thoughts of fishermen. He writes: "Every stitch in the net / is a tongue."

Sarawak is home to a diverse population of indigenous communities, totalling over forty sub-ethnic groups, broadly categorized as Dayak—including Iban (Sarawak's largest ethnic group, also known as Sea Dayak) and Bidayuh (also known as Land Dayak)—and Orang Ulu (Upriver People), encompassing 27 tribes including the Kayan, Kelabit, Kenyah, and Penan. Despite decades of unbridled logging and deforestation, the image of Sarawak as a tropical paradise of indigenous tribes and lush rainforest persists in the popular imagination of Malaysians and foreigners, many of whom view it as an exotic destination for holiday escapades. Once nicknamed "Land of the Headhunters" by British colonial officers, adventurers, and orientalists who encountered the old headhunting tradition of Iban warriors, Sarawak is affectionately referred to by locals as *Bumi Kenyalang*, "Land of the Hornbills," the majestic bird that is a shared cultural symbol among the people of Sarawak and adorns the official state emblem.

In world literature, Sarawak was for a long time known as the land of the "White Rajah" James Brooke, the first British "ruler" of Sarawak who was portrayed as a villain in Emilio Salgari's 19th century *Sandokan* swashbuckler pirate series, and who was one of Joseph Conrad's main inspirations for the titular character of his novel, *Lord Jim*. Less known to the literary world are the intricate oral traditions and material culture of the indigenous people of Sarawak—storytelling, ceremonial songs, ritual incantations, *pua kumbu* dream weaving, traditional hand-tapped tattooing—in which their complex worldviews and values are embodied and expressed. While representations of Sarawak continue to be shaped by the often incongruous accounts of outsiders and locals, the power of the outsider's gaze in defining Sarawak is gradually diminishing as indigenous communities assert their local knowledge and ways of telling, in traditional and new forms.

Grasi's poetry is a new way of telling. It deliberately roots itself in the power of orality, inscribing the transient immediacy of utterance into a palimpsest of language and meaning. It subverts the persistence of literary tropes that portray indigenous people as noble savages, by turns oppressed and exalted by a doomed humanity. Drawing potent symbolism and structure from indigenous oral traditions, Grasi's poetry does not seek to rescue, reclaim, or recast. Instead, it urges a rethinking of representations of "the indigenous," resisting sentimentalized notions of cultural identity as well as reductive binaries of tradition vs. modernity. By choosing Malay, the national language of his country, as his primary language of expression, Grasi asserts his place as a national poet, refusing to be relegated to the periphery as a "marginalized minority." By affirming the Iban, Kayan, Kelabit, and Bidayuh languages as valid vessels for contemporary expression alongside Malay, Grasi disrupts the neat categories of linguistic identity that are played out in Malaysia's politics of language.

Born in Kapit, a town by the banks of the Rajang River, to a family of Iban descent, Grasi started writing poetry at the age of 15. Urged by his reading of Malay and Indonesian poets and authors such as Usman Awang, A. Samad Said, and Chairil Anwar, Grasi embraced Malay as his own literary language. It soon struck him, however, that indigenous people were rarely represented in Malay literature. During one of our many conversations in the process of translating this book, Grasi told me, "I was reading all kinds of Malay literature. None of it spoke from the experience of Borneo's indigenous people, so I started keeping journals, writing about the lives of indigenous communities that I observed with my own eyes. This was the true beginning of my poetry." As his love for contemporary literature deepened, so did his explorations of Sarawak's indigenous languages and oral traditions, now lodged inextricably at the heart of his poetry. Grasi is uniquely placed in his organic understanding of Sarawak's vast and various indigenous communities and languages. In his day job as a school teacher, Grasi was sent to live and teach for six years among Orang Ulu communities in Baram, where he learned the Kayan, Kelabit, and Penan languages. Grasi's years with the Orang Ulu, his connection to his own Iban heritage, and his intimacy with Bidayuh culture, inform distinct yet intertwining parts of his poetic expression.

This book unfolds in three parts, each one exploring a physical, mythical, and personal topography of the poet's self. The first part, *Akui*, reaches back to Grasi's years with the Orang Ulu; it speaks of his coming of age, sexual awakening, and capricious nature. Here, Grasi intersperses his Malay with phrases of Kayan and Kelabit. The second part, *Kulleh*, invokes the presence of the Iban *pengayau* headhunters, Bujang Berani warriors, and the pantheon of gods and goddesses from their abode of *Tangsang Kenyalang*, the Hornbill's Nest. In the final section, Grasi, the poet embarks on voyages of *pimoh*, a Bidayuh dream.

My treatment of the indigenous terms and phrases in Grasi's poetry was instinctive rather than formulaic—I translated some terms from the Iban, Kayan, and Bidayuh, and in several places I deliberately left untranslated the phrases that Grasi uses as a kind of incantation, where the aurality of the phrase is paramount. I worked closely with Grasi throughout the process of translation, and we decided together which phrases to leave untranslated. In juxtaposing translated and untranslated text, we emphasize the inextricable layering of multiple languages that is characteristic of Kulleh's work. The untranslated text still signifies—the absent presence of meaning invites us to imagine, to engage in another kind of reading and listening.

"The universe arrives entangled," Grasi tell us. The distance from soil to sky is mirrored, condensed, and transmuted in the bond between the body of the poet and the spirits that inhabit "every corner" of Sarawak. The language of poetry abolishes the remoteness between this world and others—primordial rhythms transport the poet from waking reality to the underworld of *sebayan*, and paradise is only "a finger's length from the bough's eye." The *ruai*, communal corridor of an Iban longhouse, is the port of departure to an "odyssey of light lying behind the next chasm." Grasi wields his poetry like a stellar map, charting his journey through constellations of blood, memory, and personal freedom.

# BAHAGIAN 1
## AKUI

# PART 1
# AKUI

**Akui**


Sepet si jauhari
menyinsing kelikir berpelukan
manikam menangis dari bebola senja
Long Bedian.

Bersandar dagu pohon adau
siulan semilir segenggam
jantung leluhur *Ding Ngau*
meraba-raba nadi sendiri.

Jika keturunan ini
adalah anak naga,
deru sungai deras
pasti berakit di lubuk kata
paling dalam,
memuntahkan kelesuan mata.

*Isip* tumbuh selepas hujan,
nagamu tak tersinggung,
tetapi *meng ngasau akui*,
aku *akui*.

## Akui

Sun-squint on the horizon
illuminates clenched gravel,
tear-stones from dusk's eyeball at
Long Bedian.

Against the knot of the *adau* tree
the wind's rustle, heart-fist of the
ancestor of *Ding Ngau*
feeling his own pulse.

If these descendants
are the sons of dragons,
the turbulent waters
will surely drift to the deepest
word cavern
spewing a listless eye.

*Isip* leaves emerge after rain,
your dragon is unperturbed,
but *meng ngasau akui*,
I, *akui*.

## Nebula

Tirai di jendela pegun
lantai yang kaupijak
menjenguk pagi.

Udara di luar *ruai* berhimpun di jari,
sengaja kaugosok laut biru di atas
daun semesta.

180 purnama turun timbul
gerhana di tepi telinga *ikak*,
bagaimana harus aku menyentuh pelangi
yang engkau rancang terbit di hadapan dahi.

Kurempuh hujan sekali
dan harus demam
untuk bersukacita dengan alam.

Dan saat mentari menurun
jika cahayamu hanya untuk satu sanubari
mengapa kaupancar kepada semua arah?

Aku harus pergi Nebula,
odisi cahaya yang kaucari
ada di sebalik lubang lain,
bukan hanya dahaga.

*Selingut Urung* berbunyi sayu
berbalas gema
*nyalam, liveng*
*nyalam, liveng*
*ikak*.

## Nebula

Drapes hang at the startled window.
The floor you tread
catches sight of the dawn.

The air beyond the *ruai* gathers at your fingers.
Deliberately you stroke the blue sea onto
the leaf of the world.

180 full moons rise and set,
an eclipse at the edge of your ear.
How should I touch the cloud-flame
that you conjure before my brow?

I tussle with the rain
enduring fever
to revel in nature.

As the sun sinks:
if your light is meant for a single soul
why do you radiate in all directions?

I must go, Nebula.
You look for an odyssey of light
lying behind the next chasm,
not only in our thirst.

*Selingut Urung*, the nose flute, sings in
yearning echoes:
*nyalam, liveng*
*nyalam, liveng*
*ikak.*

## Dahan

Murum dan Bakun bukan sepusat,
salai babi bergantungan
petala warna tersenyum.
*Kulleh Lenge* masih lena di dahan.
*Tiga layan ko kina*:
berehatlah dalam kedamaian,
Tugang menoleh ke langit.
Jarak Eden hanya sejengkal dari
mata dahan.

## Bough

Murum and Bakun are unbound at the navel,
smoked boar hanging,
the many lips of the sky part into color.
*Kulleh Lenge*, the white-necked leopard, sleeps still on the bough.
*Tiga layan ko kina*:
sinking away into the hush of things,
Tugang turns towards the sky.
The distance to Eden is only a finger's length from
the bough's eye.

## Seekor Rusa Bernama Kalang

Pohon tebelian bergoncang
daun kering di luar rumah
ranting menyamar menjadi rusa
orkid yang dipetik
kau hadiahkan pada *Laong*
yang berkening condong
alis mata yang jatuh.

Lalu rusa mengunyah kelopak orkid,
yang kau namakan Kalang.

Terbang Kalang
Terbang Kalang
Terbang Kalang

Musim menuai bakal tiba
dagingmu disalai
kulitmu diselimut
dibungkus rapi
menjadi helai kenangan.

## A Deer Named Kalang

The *tebelian* tree shudders:
cracked leaves by the house,
sticks morphing into a deer,
the snapped orchid
you offer to the *Laong*
with the slant forehead,
the low eyebrows.

Petals gnawed at by the little deer,
which you name Kalang.

Fly Kalang
Fly Kalang
Fly Kalang

When the harvest season draws near,
your meat will be smoked
your hide shrouded
neatly bundled—
a scrap of what is remembered.

## Kelunan Harapan

*(Khas untuk Cikgu Henneser Uning Bong,*
*Guru Besar pertama suku Penan, Baram)*

Buana lang terbang
Long Main lafaz semboyan bersahutan
bergayutan orang belanda melolong
menyokong babi mencuri habuan.

Berkulit kaki
menghentak kemelut embun
pepatong hinggap di telinga
meniti denai geliga
*bek akaue medai*
*bek puun ungap*
kutinggalkan liur masam
tidak di dahan
tidak di sungai
hanya permai.

Apoi rusa belang kaki
melompat kodok
berlendir hidung
telinga mengusap mata
kautemani menari
berlari ke pondok ilmu
A Abu
B Buku.

Kejora berlari pawana batil
daun kalendar di lipat menjadi surat
kelikir mengukir janji suku terpinggir.

## Man of Hope

*(For Cikgu Henneser Uning Bong,
the first Penan headmaster in Baram)*

Long Main stirs a cacophony of sirens, the howls
of swinging Dutchmen
cheering on boars as they pillage bountiful fields
in a world where eagles fly.

Barefoot,
I grapple the chaos of mist,
a dragonfly lands on my ear
as I cross the wisdom-dirt-path:
*bek akaue medai*
*bek puun ungap*
I leave no trace of sour saliva,
only beauty
on the branch
in the river.

Apoi, stripe-footed deer,
leaps froglike
gloss-nosed
ears caressing eyes.
You dance alongside
running towards the knowledge-hut.
A Ash
B Book.

The morning star surges, a phantom wind.
Calendar leaves fold into letters
as pebbles inscribe the promises of an isolated tribe.

36 tahun, Uning yang hening
raja tanah, ya maha adil
beradu di bantal empuk
kelunan
bukan yang terakhir.

*Baram, 2006*

36 years, the placid Uning,
king of the soil, the all-just,
sleeps on a tender headrest.
A man,
not the last.

*Baram, 2006*

## Apoi dan Kalang

Aku menulis sekalung puisi
berdaun tiga di leher pohon ara
titis embun yang bermalam di kantung periuk kera
hampir pecah kerana amarahmu memancut hiba
kenapa kaupilih untuk menyamar menjadi rumput
sedang sayapmu mampu terbang bersemayam di sarang Sang
     *Tinggang*?

Apa kaumalu kerana Solomon melihat paruhmu lebih besar dari
     kelelakianmu?
Apa kaumalu kerana matamu tidak bisa berpura pura?
Apa kaumalu telur leluhurmu lebih luarbiasa dari burung lain?

Bijaknya dikau *Tinggang*,
Jatamu di puja satu keturunan
Kaupilih rusa kembar berdagu putih
Menari di sepanjang gigi sungai
Apoi dan kalang bercumbu sesama sendiri
Lupa resmi alam
Bila pipit angkuh menjodong
Walhal Apoi menjilat bibir Kalang kerana terjerat duri.

Berehat berbangku tangan
Sang *Kulleh* rimau dahan bermata tajam
mengira jarak mendayung langkah
dan mega pun
sendu,
berlalu.

## Apoi and Kalang

I write a necklace of poems
three-leafed at the nape of a fig tree.
A pool of dew at rest in the sack of a pitcher plant
almost breaks at the surge of your seething temper.
Why do you disguise yourself as grass
when your wings stir to roost in the nest of the *Tinggang*?

Are you ashamed that Solomon sees your beak as larger than
 your manhood?
Are you ashamed that your eyes cannot lie?
Are you ashamed that the eggs of your ancestors are more
 striking than others?

How wise you are, *Tinggang*,
your emblem worshipped by one people.
You follow white-bearded deer, twins
dancing along the teeth of the river.
Apoi and Kalang are busy with foreplay
forgetting nature's code.
A vain sparrow taunts them
but Apoi is only licking Kalang's thorn-tangled lips.

Head resting on his paws,
*Kulleh*, leopard of keen eyes,
reckons the distance, paddles his steps
as the clouds drift by,
grieving.

## Duri di Hujung Bibirmu

Keresahan adalah lagu
sejambak bunga terbaring lesu di kelakianmu
epitaph terpadam di dinding
kaurenung kenangan
bercawat hitam di kerusi kaki.

Berjuta-juta batu
aku rakamkan sebungkus ludahan
kautukar menjadi haruman *burak*
camar ketawa bersindir
mabok di dalam kemaluan.

Peta masa berputar
bibirmu berduri
*akei asi kui*
takkan sembuh dijilat ketika.

## A Thorn at the Edge of Your Lips

Disquiet is a song,
a spray of flowers lying listless at your manhood,
an epitaph erased from the wall.
Sheathed in black loincloth
 at the chair-feet, you sit and remember.

Millions of miles:
I chronicle a sachet of spit
that you transform into the scent of *burak* rice wine;
the dove laughs, mocking,
drunk in shame.

The map of time rotates.
Your lips are thorny:
*akei asi kui*
the lapping of time won't heal it.

## Seekor Rusa Bernama Kalang II

Matahari memanjat dagu langit
manusia bertengkar tentang filosofi
kau tinggalkan aku di *kelirieng*
rumah kematian yang berbau
mayat-mayat bergaduh

Lahiriah yang bergantungan
di siling kangkang
dijolok telunjuk
bukan oval
bukan sfera

Otak-otak bergelimpangan di meja
menunggu untuk di papan
di kepala
kau padamkan *parap* dan *takna*
yang kaucacah sendiri
di sebelah dadamu yang pucat

Berkocak darah dari pucuk naluri
disiram *bakeh*mu dengan *limo*
aku masih menghidu bau mulutmu
berwarna jingga
masih senja

Selamat jalan Kalang
*akui liveng ikak*
tanduk dan belang dagumu
menjadi atlas kenangan
kita beriring ke rumah kematian.

Di atas para sebelah utara
ada selopak air mata.

Air dari sebuah bianglala.

## A Deer Named Kalang II

The sun scales the sky's jawline
as people argue over philosophy;
you left me at the *kelirieng*,
house of the dead that stinks of
jostling corpses.

Figures hanging
from the roof of the crotch,
probed with a forefinger:
not oval
not sphere.

Brains lying strewn on the table,
heads waiting to be
thrust down;
you expunge *parap* and *takna*
that you tattooed onto
one side of your pallid chest.

Blood spurts from the primal stalk
doused by your friend with lime;
even now I smell your mouth
vermillion
still dusk.

Farewell Kalang,
*akui liveng ikak,*
your horns and tuft beard
are a memory atlas
of our procession to the house of the departed.

On the northern shelf,
where tears collect:

The waters of *bianglala*.

## Halam Ikak

Bayang-bayang
menghentakkan kepalamu
ke dinding
baluk-baluk ke udara
bernada sape bertali empat
sekeping nafas
di atas jarimu
menangis hiba

Biru dan ungu bernikah di udara
menuruni tangga langit
tergelincir ke dalam benak
kaurahsia kematianmu
di atas ranjang jenaka
*Urip anih nei kah sayu*

Ubun ke ubun
bibir ke bibir
kaumati sekali lagi
*Urip anih nei kah sayu?*

*Marudi*

## Halam Ikak

Shadows
pound your head
to the wall,
clef into the air.
Tones of a four-stringed *sape*:
a slice of breath
on your fingers
lamenting.

Blue and violet touch in the air,
descend the sky-stairs,
slip into thoughts.
You conceal your death
on this humorous bed:
*Urip anih nei kah sayu.*

Crown to crown,
lips to lips.
You die again:
*Urip anih nei kah sayu?*

*Marudi*

## Bianglala Seridan

Burung besi dari bentara
seperti pedati
menerjah hutan huma
bianglala bercerita
tinggalkan kisah itu
kabut tanah tinggi memeluk
menyelubungi kronologi keluarga Tagal
sadis pedis

*leleng, leleng uyau along leleng,*
*leleng, leleng uyau along leleng*

Bebaris padu
"Selamat datang, wahai orang Iban",
manis madu nanas dataran,
simbolik budi *Irau mekaa ngadan*,
di sebalik banjaran
pribumi penan
Ketua Kapung Long Meraan, Long Naring,
Ba Ubong,
dan pastinya Long Seridan.
ucap ubun-ubun,
tanah dan angin saksi
tanggungjawab pendidik bumi Kenyalang!

Dingin malu-malu,
Semah bertelur di batu kerangan
Sungai Magoh, raja Empurau,
Si Luhat menjerit,
*Sigu, ikan bersembunyi di kaki mu!*

## Bianglala Seridan

Iron bird of heralds,
like a cart
charging through a forested hill-paddy,
*bianglala* narrates:
leave that tale
until mist from the highland encircles
cloaking the chronology of the Tagal clan,
brutal, pained.

*leleng, leleng uyau along leleng,*
*leleng, leleng uyau along leleng*

Lined up close,
"Welcome, Iban man."
Pineapple honey-sweet from the plains,
symbol of the rite of *Irau mekaa ngadan.*
Beyond the mountains
native Penans,
village chiefs of Long Meraan, Long Naring,
Ba Ubong,
and of course Long Seridan.

Greetings from the brow,
the ground, and wind bear witness
to the task of the guru of this earth
of Kenyalang!

Cool, shy
*semah* fish spawn among shell-rocks,
Magoh River, king *empurau*,
Little Luhat calls out:
*Sigu, fish are hiding at your feet!*

*Busak bakui, dilun busak bakui, busak bakui dilun busak bakui*

Tidak semudah mengeja kata
Si Lutang, si Aning gigih mengasah eja
Sakitnya geliga bila buah epal di sebut nangka
tersenyum meresap jiwa
Mengeleng tandanya masih ada harapan.
Cuba lagi wahai anak-anak rimba!

Kepulan putih putih bahasa
musim kemarau melanda desa
Aduh, musim bersantai ria
baju seluar, besar kecil semuanya
di dobi alam semesta.
Riuh!

Si gemuk, si pendek, si kurus
dia guru juga penyelia asrama
lewat kemajuan di buletin utama
kami menadah air hujan untuk bekalan nyawa
mengeledah hutan bara
mencari calon duduk UPSR
mengubah biar sedikit
asal hati kecil mula besuara.

Rindunya,
walau asal cuba mengubah fakta
mengubah cara.
Tidak! Biar mereka selesa menjadi anak rumah *adang*
menjadi rumah tiang
tiang sejuta untuk tahun tahun mendatang.

*Busak bakui, dilun busak bakui, busak bakui dilun busak bakui*

It's not so easy to spell words.
Little Lutang, Little Aning hone their skills,
the awkward pain of calling an apple a jackfruit,
smiling. The word seeps into the psyche. Shaking one's head is a
    sign of hope still.
Try again, O children of the forest!

White white billows of language—
the dry season engulfs the countryside,
ah, season of idle pleasures,
shirts trousers, all sizes big and small,
in the laundry of the universe.
Rowdy!

Fatty, shorty, skinny,
he is both teacher and hostel supervisor.
The progress of primetime news says
we catch rainwater to give us life,
foraging in the jungle,
searching for UPSR candidates,
let change come slowly
so long as the buried heart starts talking.

Such longing,
though you tried at first to change the facts,
change their ways.
No! Let them feel at home being
children of the Adang
becoming a pillared house,
a million pillars for the years
to come.

Bersuara biarlah dari hati
walau fakta bukan merdeka setiap pesisi
cara yang ikhlas, luhur dan termateri
pasti terlerai ego dewata negeri
Sang Sarawak harus bangun,
Si Aning masih tertidur
berbantalkan jari.

*30 Ogos 2007*
*Long Meraan,*
*Baram*

Let the heart say it
although facts are not free of every corner.
Ways that are sincere, noble, inscribed
will unravel the egos of the gods of this land:
Sarawak must wake up.
Little Aning is still asleep
head pillowed on her fingers.

*30 August 2007*
*Long Meraan,*
*Baram*

# BAHAGIAN 2
# KULLEH

# PART 2
# KULLEH

## Bujang Berani

*Terutu* hujan kelabu
menghidu tengkuk ke puting
besi dan tembaga bernoda di dada
taring babi sabit terjaga
bau *munsuh* di sebelah awan.
Hampir terputus kelar kokok
ayam jantan mendabik
*Labong Bungai Nuing* dililit di kepala
terkucir beruang di luar jendela.

*Tangkung kenyalang ke ba lanjang*
*ukai di engkah ngapa*
*nanda ke aku sigi enda pulai puang*
*selabit kayau ku'ma.*

## Bujang Berani

                  Beads of gray rain
inhale nape to nipple
steel and copper flecked on the chest
boar's tusk a wakeful crescent
the enemy's scent beyond the clouds.
                  Throat half slit
the rooster shrieks and thrashes
*Labong Bungai Nuing* wrapped around the head
the bear is unsettled at the threshold.

*Tangkung kenyalang ke ba lanjang*
*ukai di engkah ngapa*
*nanda ke aku sigi enda pulai puang*
*selabit kayau ku'ma.*

## Indu Kibong I (Perempuan Penyala Lampu Tembaga)

*Ginchi-ginchi lundai bejalai,*
*minching* lampu tembaga,
bederai-derai *indu utai*
melilau mengejar gemalai
malam nan dara
perempuan tebu pemanis madu
bersimpuh bersandar pintu.

*Eh lanyi… saie eh lanyi…*
*melan-melan bungai setanggie,*
*richah ngipak perencing pegari…*
*dara pandai tampun puji*

Memetik jelaga api
bergentayangan di tingkap alam
memekik-mekik *kesindap*
menghadap *bungai* durian,
lentik jemari *Indu* menggomol lauk
buat santapan.

Ingin dirinya
dijulang seperti *Indu Dara Tinchin Temaga*
dipuja seperti kelenjar daun sireh
seputeh kapur kayangan.

Dipetiknya lagi lampu tembaga
ungka mengaru ekor
sebelah tangan bergayut di peha pokok
ranumnya syair *Kumang Peruji*
bedecit-decit ketawa tenggiling purba
*Indu* mengolah irama tak berbunyi.

## Indu Kibong (The Copper Lamp Girl)

*Ginchi-ginchi lundai bejalai,*
she carries a copper lamp as
*indu utai*, winged termites, fall and scatter
seeking out the grace
of the untouched night.
Like a sugarcane stalk, sap-sweet,
she sits, leaning against the door.

*Eh lanyi… saie eh lanyi…*
*melan-melan bungai setanggie,*
*richah ngipak perencing pegari…*
*dara pandai tampun puji*

Igniting flame soot—floating, aimless
eyes at nature's window,
*kesindap* bats shriek
by the durian flower.
Kneading petals between fingers backward-bent,
*Indu* prepares a meal offering.

She longs to be lifted like *Indu Dara Tinchin Temaga*
to be worshipped like the veins of betel leaves,
white as the chalk of *kayangan*.

Again she lights the copper lamp,
the rain weeps,
a gibbon claws at its rump,
one arm dangling from the tree's thigh,
how lush the ode of *Kumang Peruji*.
The screeching laugh of the ancient pangolin,
seeing *Indu* make only a soundless melody.

Aku tidak dapat ketawa,
Aku juga belum mampu menangis,
Aku kemudian.

*Ukai nya naka uleh merap tajau pesaka raja,*
*Mina ulih nguan ke pesaka raja, dudi ari sigi nenggam menua.*
Dunia nyata.

Dunia nyata peturun *Indu Kibong*.

*Kuching, 2017*

I cannot laugh,
I cannot weep yet,
later, later.

*Ukai nya naka uleh merap tajau pesaka raja,*
*Mina ulih nguan ke pesaka raja, dudi ari sigi nenggam menua.*
The seen world.

The seen world, daughters of *Indu Kibong.*

*Kuching, 2017*

## Icit

Bersenyawa embun dara
membalut kebal bulu Ungka
berpeluk intim *empeliau* tua
melilit betina yang masih ada.

Sa, dua, tiga, empat, lima, enam, tujuh!
Tuai Kulleh berkumat kumit,
*Nadai ngawa, nadai apa,*
*burung jaik nadai di dinga.*

Membelit *nyabor*
*sangkuh* di julang, perahu di goyang
belum bangun laknat *kerengit-kerengit* miang
dara Bangan berpesan
kumpul buah *engkabang*.

Berkepul-kepul *Semakau Apong*,
berbasa basi
*mupuk aku.*

Belantara Katibas
kalau di kira puaka Pelagus
seraga mata sudah disalai.
Nanga Anchau masih berjanji
suku Memaloh suku Rejang,
Iban Song, Iban Wong,
cukup piring maka sempurnalah huma.

## Icit

Fresh dew on the fur
of mating gibbons, they
clutch close as the old *empeliau* male
circles the sole female.

*Sa, dua, tiga, empat, lima, enam, tujuh!*
Kulleh's head muttering:
*Nadai ngawa, nadai apa,*
*burung jaik nadai di dinga.*

Kulleh sheaths his *nyabor* sword,
raises his spear, pushes his boat through the water.
While vile sandflies are still sleeping,
the young girl, Bangan, asks him
to gather *engkabang* fruit.

Smoke of *apong* palm tobacco,
talking without saying,
*mupuk aku.*

Wilderness of Katibas,
if the curse of Pelagus is true,
a basket of eyes will be smoked.
Nanga Anchau still promises
the Memaloh and Rejang tribes,
Iban Song, Iban Wong,
abundant offerings will
ensure a good harvest.

Lalu diterjahnya jeram,
Mayau dan Angkabang berkeringat sebesar kerang
Aki Kulleh memejam mata
"Sabar bujang,
sekejap lagi perahu ke seberang.
*Aram!*"

Lang bejawang pun berlagu
Lang sengalang pun bercerita
digalur pada nama,
Kulleh Sulung Kulleh bongsu.
Pesan Aki,

"*Bejalailah* sehingga ke China,
siling mereka adalah baju kita,
belajar lah sehingga ke Amerika,
pensel mereka adalah *Tugal* kita."
Hasil benih campuran Rejang,
mewarisi gelar bukan sebarang.
Kain *Kebat, lampit* Perak,
Buah pelaga, *Rawai* Tembaga,
*Selampai Buri Baju Taya*,
Gelang *Buluk Gerunong Siong*.

Apak, Aki,
purnama ini dikisahkan
Nanga Anchau dalam atlas
buah *engkabang* di dalam cerita
legasi Kulleh menjunjung setia.

*Nanga Anchau, Song*

Head-on against the rapids,
the brothers Mayau and Angkabang drip sweat-beads as big as
    clams.
Aki Kulleh shuts his eyes,
"Be patient, my sons,
soon the boat will cross.
Aram!"

Lang Bejawang sings,
Lang Sengalang narrates,
knotted by name
Kulleh the eldest, Kulleh the youngest,
Aki says,

"*Bejalailah* all the way to China,
their coins are our clothes,
study all the way to America,
their pencils are our *tugal* sticks."
Fruit of the mixed seeds of Rejang, a youth
inheriting titles is not to be taken lightly.
*Kebat* cloth, silver *lampit*,
carnelian stone, copper *rawai*,
*Selampai Buri Baju Taya,*
bracelet of *Buluk Gerunong Siong.*

*Apak, Aki,*
this full moon charts
Nanga Anchau on the atlas,
charts the *engkabang* fruit in the story,
charts the legacy of Kulleh upheld in loyalty.

*Nanga Anchau, Song*

43

## Aku Belum Lesi

Benang yang di muntahkan
dari bibir *mulong*,
menjadi jumud tidak mengalir lagi,
kumbahan reput di dahan.

Menjelma rumit angkasaraya
tidak mampu menghidu haruman syurga,
seperti ludahan *Raja Sempulang Gana*
mara kering di udara.

Anak ribut meronta
di hening *Sendi Dara Anja*,
Pua rayong berbunyi *Lang Jawang*
jadi joget dalam Publika,
tabloid udara—lukisan jelmaan pengantara *Tali Kebayu*,
diriwayatkan; hidup
seperti aku tidak mahu *lesi* di tinta.

*Betong, Sarawak*

44

### I, Unfaded

Thread thrown up
from the *mulong* worm's lips
grows stiff, no longer flows.
Waste decays on the branch.

The universe arrives entangled.
We cannot sense the fragrance of paradise
like the spit of *Raja Sempulang Gana*
lurching dry in the air.

Child of the storm flailing
in the silence of *Sendi Dara Anja*.
*Pua rayong* sings the incantation of *Lang Jawang*
into a *joget* at Publika.
Tabloids of air—etching the form of the medium *Tali Kebayu*.
Narrated, alive.
As if I do not want to fade in ink.

*Betong, Sarawak*

45

**Sendi**

Pekat gelap terjurai
di leher jinjang,
bana berkepul-kepul
dari batu kemenyan.

Sutera rambut membelakangi
tubuh giur kuning langsat,
tersadai di bahu malam.

*Asai ke meda bali berinjan,*
*ukai gak,*
*bisi baka bali belumpung,*
*ukai gak,*
*engka ya di sebut kumbu rayong,*
*tauka kumbu muau,*
*serta bisi gak baka bandau nulang.*

*Bunsu* angin dan *bunsu* ribut
bekecamuk,
meletup letup di dahi
jari menenun,
menusuk setiap gambar yang marah,
menyumpah ayam berkokok sebelum subuh.

Di bayangi kenyalang,
*ketupung* yang becok
berkicau di dahan.
*Ensera* ini bukan hikayat petang petang.

Berpancar kilat halilintar
memecah mimpi,
bertempiaran lalang,
*Niang Inik* Bangan berkata,

### Sendi

Dense, dark, unraveling
at the slender nape,
her birthmark of smoke
from *kemenyan* stones.

Hair-silk down the back of an
alluring body, *langsat* yellow,
sprawled on night's shoulder.

*Asai ke meda bali berinjan,*
*ukai gak,*
*bisi baka bali belumpung,*
*ukai gak,*
*engka ya di sebut kumbu rayong,*
*tauka kumbu muau,*
*serta bisi gak baka bandau nulang.*

Spirits of wind and storm
rage wild,
erupting at her brow.
Her fingers weaving,
she stabs each angry image,
curses the rooster that crows before dawn.

What she thought was the *kenyalang*
is the *ketupung*, omen bird,
screeching on the branch.
This *ensera* is no bedtime story.

Lighting and thunderclap
break her dreams,
windswept *lalang*;
*Niang Inik* Bangan says,

47

*baik pua tok Jang,*
*senira benang tengkudu,*
*tikar sapat beribu,*
*kupan papan chalu.*

Menoleh Sendi
menyeringai gigi
senyum berlagu.

*Nya baru terkinsit pintu langit,*
*baka wit kemudi tendan*
*nya baru bekeredu bintang buyu,*
*mandus langu kenunsung tanam,*
*bekedura bintang tiga,*
*besemaya enggau anak mensia nangkal tegalan.*

Sendi,
mimpi-mimpi yang dipeluk,
mencari puisi dari hutan,
ritma dari *sebayan*,
kasidah dari bunian,
tiada lagi lagu kaucerita
*pua* ditenun,
serpihan batu pelaga,
bederai beribu.

*Pulai* Sendi, *pulai*.

*baik pua tok Jang,*
*senira benang tengkudu,*
*tikar sapat beribu,*
*kupan papan chalu.*

*Sendi* turns,
bares her teeth,
grinning and singing.

*Nya baru terkinsit pintu langit,*
*baka wit kemudi tendan*
*nya baru bekeredu bintang buyu,*
*mandus langu kenunsung tanam,*
*bekedura bintang tiga,*
*besemaya enggau anak mensia nangkal tegalan.*

*Sendi*,
these dreams we carry,
seek poems from the jungle,
rhythms from *sebayan*,
qasidahs from *bunian*.
There are no songs left for you to sing.
She has woven the *pua*,
the Carnelian cracks
into a thousand shards.

*Pulai* Sendi, *pulai*.

## Manjong

*Sangkuh* dan *ilang* yang memenggal kepala
tidak seperti mancis
membakar seruang taman.

Taman karya, taman tulisan
Taman potret, taman lukisan
Taman hati.

*Pengayau*

Kepala musuh yang dijulang
dihirup *ai jalong*
*lekapadi* dari tanah adan.

Tujuh kali kau*manjong*
tangan kanan mengayau
kiri kaudakap
pucuk naluri lelaki
hujan panas.

*5 Jun, Selepas Gawai*

## Manjong

*Sangkuh* spear, *ilang* sword to sever heads
unlike a match
that scorches the whole garden.

Garden of rhapsody, of chant,
of portraits, of etchings:
heart-garden.

*Pengayau*

The enemy's head thrust high,
the taste of *ai jalong*,
*lekapadi* from the hills.

Seven times you sound the war cry,
right hand headhunting,
left clutching
your primal stalk
in the sun-rain.

*5 June, after Gawai*

**Ibun**

Cupola antara langit
kubah yang terletak di antara pembahagian
garis *Sengalang* dan maerhanis
menyahut deru-deru tembaga loceng
terngiang-ngiang becok mulut *Ketupung*
besok dipermandikan,
cukup 12 purnama telur jantan.

Nama puji nama berani
*Inik Andan Rabong Menua,*
*Inik Indi Rabong Ari,*
menyampai tirakat
duka murka masih di dada
terlarang kasih *Sera Gunting*
dan sunti Si *Endu Chempaka Tempurung Alang*,
jangan diulangi lagi.

Sabda,

*Dini alai nuan Seramugah,*
*nya orang ke ngempu tanah,*
*ngelala iya ke jaik iya ke manah, ke betuai alai buma.*
*Dini nuan Seragindi,*
*nya orang ke ngemata ke lubang ai, dalam enda anchik-anchik,*
*iya ke nyengala perebeni mayuh nanga*

Sebelum separa badan,
gesel air dara sungai Menua:
Ohh Hansi anak lelaki tegap bediri
Bujang anak bujang berani mati
Yen anak matang bijak berdikari
Sisok anak sopan pekerti elok
Wat anak jantan berjiwa seni
Aspa dara kebal perindu puisi
Kulleh anak gigih dalam bermimpi

## Ibun

Cupola suspended in the sky,
dome between the line that divides
*Sengalang* and the crowds
responding to the roar of copper bells,
the prattling clangor of *Ketupung*'s mouth.
Tomorrow a river baptism—
male seeds arrive at 12 full moons.

Names of praise, names of bravery:
*Inik Andan Rabong Menua,*
*Inik Indi Rabong Ari,*
name as incantation.
Sorrow and rage still tear at the breast,
the forbidden love of *Sera Gunting*,
the maiden *Endu Chempaka Tempurung Alang*.
Don't repeat it.

It is said,

*Dini alai nuan Seramugah,*
*nya orang ke ngempu tanah,*
*ngelala iya ke jaik iya ke manah, ke betuai alai buma.*
*Dini nuan Seragindi,*
*nya orang ke ngemata ke lubang ai, dalam enda anchik-anchik,*
*iya ke nyengala perebeni mayuh nanga*

Before half your body
grazes the Menua river's untouched waters, listen—
Oh, Hansi, young man standing tall.
Bujang, warrior's son, unafraid of death.
Yen, seasoned hunter, independent, wise.
Sisok, refined youth who is shaped by noble character.
Wat, strong man possessed by art's spirit.
Aspa, impenetrable woman who yearns for poetry like a distant lover.
Kulleh, child adrift in dreams.

*Genselan* dirai
biar ubun-ubun dititis
embun suci
cukup purnama dimamah janji.

Oh tanah
beri sembah mereka *bejalai*
Oh dunia
beri hadiah mereka jelajah,
Oh air
biar mengalir ke pelosok terpanggil
terpilih di antara yang dipilih
legasi *Gerasi Nading*
*Bujang Berani Kempang*,
memeluk mimpi belia-belia alpa
dari Rejang bertemu di Batu Kitang
susur galur Buluh Antu hingga Skrang
belantara Nyelitak serta Lundu berombak tenang.

Tujuh dewa *tansang kenyalang*,
tujuh menantu Tuhan *Sengalang*
*Ketupong, Beragai, Pangkas,*
*Embuas, Kelabu Papau dan Burung Malam*, serta *Bejampung*.
berkelana dari mana ke sana,
Bumbok, Pulau Pinang,
terus ke Belanda,
merentas Andaman,
lautan Baltic ke Amsterdam.

*Bejalai* kisah dari cupola
saksi adat mandi sungai Menua
*Ibun* bergema,
dijaga.

*Den Haag 2016*

We offer *genselan*.
Let our crowns be anointed with
sacred dew.
The moon is heavy with our promises.

Oh earth,
bless their *bejalai*.
Oh world,
give them a place to explore.
Oh water,
let them be carried to secret corners, summoned
among the chosen few.
Legacy of *Gerasi Nading*
*Bujang Berani Kempang*.
Idle youth embracing dreams
from Rejang to meet in Batu Kitang,
bloodlines from Buluh Antu to Skrang,
the wilderness of Nyeliak to the calm tides of Lundu.

Seven gods of *tansang kenyalang*,
seven kin of the god *Sengalang*:
*Ketupong, Beragai, Pangkas,*
*Embuas, Kelabu Papau, Burung Malam*, and *Bejampung*;
wandering from where to there—
Bumbok, the island of Penang,
then to Holland,
across the Andaman,
the Baltic Sea to Amsterdam.

*Bejalai* tale from the sky vault,
witness the bathing ritual at Menua river.
*Ibun* resounds,
watched over.

*The Hague 2016*

55

## Jangan

Menganyam hijau langit
*ensurai* mengurai dari pohon
menari di atas angin kencang
sireh berbisik di kaki
Jangan pergi,
Jangan pergi.

*Sera Gunting* bercerita dengan Aki
sumbang mahram itu akil
pada rerambut dara kudus
di atas tubuhnya
Jangan caci,
Jangan caci.

**Don't**

Weaving sky-green,
*ensurai* unfurls from the tree,
dances on the high winds,
*sireh* whispering at the toes
don't leave,
don't leave.

*Sera Gunting* tells stories to Aki:
incest as puberty
at the hair of the sacred virgin,
upon her body
don't tease,
don't tease.

## Lorong Tong Sang

Malar liar *mimosa pudica*
permaidani hujan *chelap*
rumput meraba keting kaki
berjengket jengket
menolak pagar tua berlagu cello putus tali.

Beriring ampai-ampai kain sarong
batik serikin,
celana kiki lala bergelimpangan longlai
menari ditiup petang.

Suram setiap pesisi
plot jingga, kuning tanah
dan jendela.
Benak berhutang rindu
jarang melupai ruang lohong.

Cawan dan gelas bermonolog
bersyair tentang nama mereka
termasuk kalendar kertas Cina,
10 Februari 1987.

Perabot, bingkai dan dinding kipas
ketawa berdecit-decit
tikus tanah mendapat habuan dapur
sofa cudroy hijau delima—
ada lorekan kecil tangan-tangan nakal.

Mak mengiring aku ke seluruh rumah
gelas berpuisi
garpu berpantun
kain sarong bergurindam.

*berisik amat dik, jang*
*Apak dik udah ke Belaga.*

## Lorong Tong Sang

*Mimosa pudica*, wild perennial,
carpet in cool rain—
grass caresses your heels
as you tip-toe.
The old fence cries like a broken-stringed cello.

Strung up, drowsy: sarong cloth,
*batik serikin*,
Kiki Lala underwear strewn,
swaying in evening's breath.

Every corner a drab
orange plot, yellow land,
window.
Thought-tides of longing,
stalked by a memory of the abyss.

Monologue of cup and glass,
singing a *syair* of their names,
the Chinese paper calendar reads:
10 February 1987.

Furniture, picture frames, wall fan,
chirping laughter
of rats with their kitchen bounty,
corduroy sofa pomegranate green—
scribbles of naughty hands.

My mother follows me through the house:
glasses make poetry,
forks recite *pantun*,
sarongs sing *gurindam*.

*Berisik amat dik, jang*
*Apak dik udah ke Belaga.*

59

Bertatih anak kecil
mahu setampan dia.
ubun-ubun suam peluh masam,
tidak banyak celoteh, gagap
masih terkebil-kebil pongah,
anak bujang Mak.

Dia menjinjing sekampit beras
ringan sebelah tangan
berceloteh tetap *mutap*.

Aku pulang dulu
tidak mungkin datang lagi,
tak akan memeluk silam.
Erat-erat dakapan,
"*Mak, enda aku pulai kituk agi*
*aku diau din*, bersama kamu dan mereka."
1 February 2017,
sore tadi di hujung talian,
*Enda betah kitak aku*,
—33 tahun.

The child waddles,
wants to grow into a charming older self,
has a crown warm with sour sweat.
He doesn't talk much, he stutters,
Mother's son
still blinking innocently.

She carries a bag of rice,
light in one hand,
nagging away, *mutap*.

I will go now,
I won't come back,
won't insist on remembering.
A close embrace,
*Mak, enda aku pulai kituk agi*
*aku diau din,* with you and them.
1 February 2017,
this afternoon on the phone
*Enda betah kitak aku*
—33 years.

## Telaiku, Kenyalang

Gunung, sungai dan halilintar
bersahutan semilir,
embun menitik dari daun
gumpalan gomulus berubah warna.
Kau manusia pertama?
*Ngirup ai ari dunya.*

Merah, hitam dan putih purba
kau dan aku tetap sama
kita bertengkar mungkar
berkongsi setitik air
dari petala.

Lari ke sungai bertemu *antu*
lari ke laut bertandang taufan,
sembunyi dari dosa.
Zebra, *uduk*, semut,
Iceland, Tokyo, Jakarta dan kita
tiada rahsia.

Kepak mengibas
mengetuk *teresang* kita.
*Telai*ku
cerita,
Kenyalang.
Tinggi ke awan.

*Sanhill, Sibu*

### Tell Me, Kenyalang

Mountains, rivers, lightning
reply to the call of breeze.
Dew spills down the fronds,
cumulus clouds turning color:
Are you the first man?
*Ngirup ai ari dunya.*

Red, black, primordial white—
you and I stay the same,
we argue,
share a drop of water
from the sky's crest.

Run to the river to meet *antu*,
run to the sea to play in typhoons,
hiding from sin.
Zebras, dogs, ants,
Iceland, Tokyo, Jakarta, and us:
no secrets.

Wings striking
against our *teresang*.
Tell me stories,
*Kenyalang*,
high beyond the clouds.

*Sanhill, Sibu*

# BAHAGIAN 3
# GRASI

# PART 3
# GRASI

## Pimoh di Tingkap Longit

Andromeda tergantung angkuh,
kuhulur tangan untuk mencapai debuan *pimoh*
berterbangan di sekitar minda
yang tumbuh jadi bunga,
yang mencambah jadi kejora
yang terkubur jadi nisan
yang melumpur jadi ingatan.

Bulan membentuk pasang dan surut
Setiap laut merasa dirgahayunya yang sederhana.
ada merak mengibas ekor,
ada *kasuong* menjerit manja
ada kalau percaya.

Suedang dan Sa' bertepuk tangan
babainya menyanyi salah melodi
di tingkap kecil malam semalam
pintu *longit* terbuka,
bersorak sorai jubah pujian.

*Sanhill, Sibu*

66

## Pimoh at the Sky's Window

Andromeda hangs overhead, arrogant:
My hand reaches for the *pimoh* dream-dirt
floating through the mind
that grows into flowers,
that swells into Venus,
that buries into stone,
that muddies into memory.

The moon summons the ebb and flow,
every sea feels it—simple, majestic.
There's a peacock flashing its tail,
a hound yelping for attention,
they are there, if you believe.

Last night, Suedang and Sa' clapped
as *babai* sang the wrong melody.
And at the small window,
the sky's gateway cracked open:
rapture and robes of praise.

*Sanhill, Sibu*

## Koh dan Canaria

Kota aneh
angin belari kencang
palma pasung
camar melayang-layang
kutepuk buih laut menjadi awan
kuda putih dan papilon bangsawan
mengajuk mata dayakku yang tenggelam

deretan pasir membentuk duyung
artisan melakar
buih-buih ke taman asmara

kalau Canaria mampu berpuisi
Koh meninggalkan *sirat*nya
dan berlari ke Antartika.

*Las Palmas*

## Koh and Canaria

Bizarre town,
wind raging swift,
motionless palms,
seagulls hovering.
I clap sea spray into clouds,
royal white horses and papillon
mimic my drowning *dayak* eyes.

Sand dunes form a mermaid,
an artisan sketches
sea foam into gardens of pleasure.
If Canaria wrote poems
Koh would leave behind his *sirat*
and flee to Antarctica.

*Las Palmas*

69

**Ensurai gugur di Narita**


Di setiap lopak yang membentuk jalan
tersembunyi secalit embun
kaujumpa di setiap pintu bandara.

Kerdip buruj yang kaurenung
dari rumah tinggi kota metropolis
mengingatkan jatuhnya *bungai ensurai*
di atas *perabong*,
dan kaugenggam jantungku
pada tangkal hati,
berterbangan nafas ketakutan
jatuh ke lautan.

Bait naratif kau yang berbau arak
hanya sejengkal mata
saat Soju yang kaurenung berdiri
mekar di atas meja.

Malam cerah,
di bandara lain,
sakura belum musim,
kita melihat *ensurai* gugur
di Narita.


*Kuching*

## Ensurai Falling in Narita

Every pothole in the street's curve
hides a dew stain
you found at every departure gate.

The flicker of constellations you see
from a metropolis high rise
reminds you of *ensurai* flowers falling
onto *perabong*,
you grasp at my heart
as if it were a talisman,
frightened breath flying
plunging to the sea.

The lines of your narrative smell of rice wine—
it's just the distance of our eyes
when the soju you gaze at stands
erect on the table.

The night is clear
at other airports,
it's not yet sakura season:
we watch *ensurai* falling
in Narita.


*Kuching*

## Raan

Aku *raan* sebuah mimpi
Aku *raan* sebuah peta
Kau alunkan lengkap Taize
harum dari tingkap gereja kecil bonda Maria.

Kau sirami kegusaran
bunga-bunga berduri yang melewati setiap igau manusia
tak mungkin kaurebah
kerana kau turut serta bernyanyi dengan megah
tangan malaikat kecil untukku
aku persembahkan
buat mu
sampai adanya nanti.

Kita, *raan* sampai adanya nanti.

*Bumbok*

## Raan

I *raan* a dream.
I *raan* a map.
You intone the Taize, whole—
fragrant from the window of the chapel of Mother Mary.

You douse the wrath
of thorn flowers that pass through every delirium.
You won't give in,
you join the exalted singing.
I present the hand of a small angel to you,
for you,
until it comes.

Us, *raan* until it comes.

*Bumbok*

73

## Pasun Menyalak

Gerimis menurun,
lalang melayu di tepian ara.
Grasi mengangkang mendongak ke belakang
anak *mensia* tertidur di jelapang.

Ular berambus ke sarang,
kulitnya tercalar terkena batang.
Kenapa kau sembunyi?

Melolong dan terus melolong
irama bergema daun
juga turut berdiam.

"*Igat*, mari pulang"
"*Igat*, mari pulang"
"*Igat*, mari…"

## Pasun Barking

Drizzle,
*lalang* wilting by the fig grove.
Grasi sits with legs stretched open, looks back
at the human child asleep in the rice barn.

A snake slinks off to its nest,
its skin gets snagged by a branch:
why are you hiding?

Howling and howling again
as the echo song of the leaves
falls silent.

"*Igat*, come home."
"*Igat*, come home."
"*Igat*, come ..."

## Lelaki dan Bulan

Lubang di jantung awan
dijahit sulam perawan
angin menjadi senja
menanti merah mampir ke petang
selimut gersang
meruntun rawan di geliga dalam
basahnya embun
di tepian pehamu

Kamu lelaki yang menggoda Bulan
Kamu lelaki yang menggoda Bulan
Kamu lelaki yang menggoda Bulan

*malem*

## Man and Moon

Hollow in the cloud-heart
embroidered into virgin flesh.
The wind tosses into twilight
as we wait for the approach of evening-red.
Unadorned robe
tugging the restless thought-drift.
Wetness of dew
at the shore of your thighs,
waves murmur.

You, man who lures the moon,
man who lures the moon,
who lures the moon:

*night.*

## Semalam di Rian Batang

Gong berbunyi pilu
semalau berkicau tanpa malu
bertenggek di ampaian seperti tercekik
pinang nibong.

Pohon di sepanjang jalan
bersoal sesama taulan
mahu bertanya belansungkawa
bukit Bengunan hiba tak menoleh,
daun yang renyuk pun tiada bunyi,
sepi.

Di kaki tangga,
nafas terikat, jantung tertinggal di kota,
deretan kain Pua di takbir menjadi *sapat*.
kemana harus ku unjurkan kaki,
berlagu bersama mereka mengetuk *tanah midang*.

*dik indai lapa nuan beguai pegi,*
*agi belala begulai bebuti,*
*dik indai lapa meh nuan lesi,*
*ninggal ka kami kediri, nadai orang ngemata agi,*
*dik indai ahh*

Tiung pun berhenti menari,
petang yang gelap, gemawan jatuh di tepi pipi.
terpana masa sebentar,
bahu di runtun melawat kebenaran
sebingkai jasad yang anggun
tersadai di tepian anak-anaknya
bersilih bahu,
mengenggam harapan untuk terus berjalan.

## One Night at Rian Batang

A gong strikes, melancholic,
and magpies perch on the clothesline
chattering shamelessly, as if choking
on areca nuts.

Along the road, trees
ask each other
who has departed.
Bukit Begunan weighs down, does not turn,
the crumpled leaves everywhere are mute,
desolate.

Our breath is bound at the foot
of the stairs, our hearts cast off in the town,
rows of *pua* cloth hanging as *sapat*.
Where should I stretch out my legs,
to sing with them, to approach *tanah midang*?

*"dik indai lapa nuan beguai pegi,*
*agi belala begulai bebuti,*
*dik indai lapa meh nuan lesi,*
*ninggal ka kami kediri, nadai orang ngemata agi,*
*dik indai ahh"*

The mynahs stop playing,
dusk clouds tumble by your cheek.
Stunned for a moment,
dragged inside to see the frame of
a poised body
supine beside her children who stand
shoulder to shoulder,
grappling with resolve to keep living.

Sayup bintang yang bersembunyi
di ruai Rian Batang
di lipat elok
untuk kekuatan
hari-hari lain, kemudian.

Sepasang kebaya, sebuah doa,
layu dari pandangan
hanya kenangan
ketika pusaranya di peluk,
rindu berulang.

*Untuk Raygyna dan Imelda,*
*Kenangan dalam kedamaian*
*(Puan Imbong Anak Kilat 20 Disember 1960–3 February 2014)*

The faint glow of lurking stars
above the *ruai* of Rian Batang,
folded and kept,
for strength
in days to come.

A *kebaya*, a prayer,
fading from sight
into memory.
When they clasp her gravestone,
the longing surges again.

*For Raygyna and Imelda,*
*in loving memory of Puan Imbong Anak Kilat*
*(December 20, 1960–February 3, 2014)*

## Jala

Jala-jala yang robek
ikan baung sinis
sungai juga kurang pasti
kodok-kodok saling bertanya
kalau bukan ke sungai kerana berdayung.

Setiap jahitan jala
ada bahasa.

**Net**

Tattered nets.
*Baung* fish are caustic,
even the river is unsure.
Toads ask if the fishermen
have come not just to boat.

Every stitch in the net
is a tongue.

## Kapal Kertas Simongi

Kompas awan berpetakan aurora
langit purba yang tidak pernah berubah
zenith dan nadir adalah pasangannya.

Kapal kertas berlayar megah
*onak kopot* meniarap mengira *ikien*
bersembunyi di batu
mengocak jenaka melihat manusia.

Terus mengalir sungai
tanpa mengira amukan lipan berkerja
pokok bergoncang
*samak*nya menangis
lengan anaknya baru tumbuh sedepa
di sembelih tanpa suara.

Di sidang himpunan,
orang-orang bersalaman
sekulit lengan yang di gerudi semalam
menjadi sepucuk puisi.

Kapal kertas *Simongi* berlayar lagi.

*Adelaide, November*

### The Paper Boat of Simongi

The cloud compass is steered by an aurora —
ancient sky that does not change,
counterpart of zenith and nadir.

A paper boat sails, regal.
A child, *onak kopot*, sprawls out, counts the fish
hiding among rocks
teasing each other, watching people.

The river runs on,
indifferent to bulldozers running amok.
Trees shaking,
*samak* weeping:
her child's arm is now just a stump,
silently butchered.

At the gathering place,
people greet each other.
The bark of a limb, freshly drilled,
becomes a poem.

The paper boat of *Simongi* sails again.

*Adelaide, November*

**Nota untuk Pokok**


Kemandanian leluhur setiap anutan
adalah kasih sayang
nan membentuk zigot
cerita pelbagai warna dihentam petir halilintar
hujan monsoon mengubah Banda Acheh.

Kendati pengakhiran yang muncul biasan warna.
Mereka,
dari rahim yang sama
dari penyatuan perkahwinan sivil
dari baptisan diosis
dari azan Yahweh
padi dari *Sempulang Gana*
relung cahaya Vishnu.

Wahai pokok,
setiap yang di hantar
pasti pulang kembali
sama Adam, Selimah, Jalin, Imbong dan Waima.


*Nieuwe Kerk, Delft 2016*

## Notes for the Trees

Ancestors of every belief
are a kind of love:
a point of origin,
stories of all shades, lashed by thunder and lightning,
the monsoon that transfigures Banda Acheh.

Though their end arrives in a vast spectrum,
they are
from the same womb:
from a union of civil marriage,
from a diocesan baptism,
from Yahweh's call to prayer,
paddy from *Sempulang Gana*,
Vishnu's grotto of light.

O trees,
every being who is sent
will surely return,
with Adam, Selimah, Jalin, Imbong, and Waima.

*Nieuwe Kerk, Delft 2016*

# Glossary

**Kenyalang**  hornbill, specifically the rhinoceros hornbill  *IBAN*
(*Buceros rhinoceros*). The Kenyalang is an important cultural
symbol for the Dayak tribes of Sarawak, who believe the bird to be
a messenger between the human world and the celestial realm.

### 7  AKUI

**akui**  I  *KAYAN*

**Ding Ngau**  a male name, usually for someone of high tribal hierarchy  *KAYAN*

**isip**  a kind of leaf, scientific name *Phacelophrymium maximum*, often  *KELABIT*
used to wrap rice in the Bario region of Sarawak

**meng ngasau akui**  "leave me alone"  *KAYAN*

### 9  NEBULA

**ruai**  the common space that runs the length of a Sarawak long house  *IBAN*

**Selingut Urung**  a Kayan nose flute  *KAYAN*

**nyalam**  love  *KAYAN*

**liveng**  longing  *KAYAN*

**ikak**  you  *KAYAN*

### 11  BOUGH

**Murum and Bakun**  areas in Belaga, Sarawak

**Kulleh Lenge**  white-necked leopard  *KENYAH*

**Tiga layan ko kina**  "look after yourself"  *KENYAH*

**Tugang**  the name of a boy  *KENYAH*

### 13  A DEER NAMED KALANG

**Kalang**  a Kayan name  *KAYAN*

**tebelian**  a hardwood tree found throughout Borneo, scientific name  *MALAY*
*Eusideroxylon zwageri*

**Laong**  a term for a girl  *KAYAN*

## MAN OF HOPE 15

**bek akaue medai / bek puun ungap** "I'm not afraid, there are no bad     PENAN
   spirits here"

**Apoi** a Kayan name     KAYAN

## APOI AND KALANG 19

**Tinggang** hornbill     KAYAN

**Kulleh** leopard     KENYAH

## A THORN AT THE EDGE OF YOUR LIPS 21

**burak** rice wine     KAYAN

**akei asi kui** "I'm sorry"     KAYAN

## A DEER NAMED KALANG II 23

**kelirieng** Kayan totem pole     KAYAN

**parap & takna** Kayan sacred chants     KAYAN

**akui liveng ikak** "I miss you"     KAYAN

**bianglala** an old term for rainbow     MALAY

## HALAM IKAK 25

**halam ikak** your heart     KAYAN

**sape** a traditional lute of the Orang Ulu, particularly the Kayan and     MALAY
   Kenyah communities

**Urip anih nei kah sayu** "things will get better"     KAYAN

## BIANGLALA SERIDAN 27

**Bianglala Seridan** The rainbow of Seridan. Seridan refers to Long     MALAY
   Seridan, a Kelabit settlement in the Miri division of Sarawak.

**leleng, leleng uyau along leleng** a traditional song of the Orang     KELABIT
   Ulu, usually sung during the welcoming dance

**Irau mekaa ngadan** a name changing ritual of the Kelabit people     KELABIT

**semah** a freshwater fish known in English as semah mahseer or river     MALAY
   carp, scientific name *Tor douronensis*

**empurau** a species of mahseer fish native to Sarawak, referred to by     MALAY
   indigenous Sarawak communities as "king of the river," scientific
   name *Tor tambroides*

**Busak bakui, dilun busak bakui** a traditional Kelabit song, usually sung     KELABIT
   by children when they gather ferns in the jungle

**UPSR** Malaysia's national primary school Standard Six examination

rumah adang    long house                                                      KELABIT

sigu    A child's way of prouncing the Malay word *cikgu*, "teacher."          MALAY

## 35    BUJANG BERANI

Bujang Berani    brave warrior                                                 MALAY

terutu    drizzle                                                              IBAN

munsuh    enemy                                                                IBAN

Labong Bungai Nuing    cloth wrapped around the head                           IBAN

Tangkung kenyalang ke ba lanjang / ukai di engkah ngapa / nanda ke aku         IBAN
     sigi enda pulai puang / selabit kayau ku'ma    "the hornbill's beak on
     this headdress / it is not placed there arbitrarily / a sign that I will not
     return empty handed / the headhunter's basket I carry"

## 37    INDU KIBONG

Indu Kibong    girl of the mosquito net canopy, in this poem she guards a      IBAN
     copper lamp

Ginchi-ginchi lundai bejalai    "Walking carefully and gracefully"             IBAN

minching    to carry                                                           IBAN

indu utai    a winged insect                                                   IBAN

Eh lanyi saie eh lanyi...    "a copper bell sounds in the distance, as the     IBAN
     young woman waits for the break of dawn"

kesindap    bat                                                                IBAN

Indu Dara Tinchin Temaga    symbol of an idealized young woman                 IBAN

kayangan    the celestial realm                                                MALAY

Kumang Peruji    a young woman who is praised                                  IBAN

Ukai nya naka uleh    "today you look after your heritage, tomorrow you        IBAN
     inherit the world"

## 41    ICIT

Icit    grandson                                                               MALAY

Empeliau    gibbon                                                             IBAN

Sa, dua, tiga, empat, lima, enam, tujuh!    "One, two, three, four, five, six, MALAY
     seven!"

Nadai ngawa, nadai apa, burung jaik nadai di dinga    "It's alright, it's      IBAN
     nothing, there's no bad omen"

nyabor    an Iban sword                                                        IBAN

sangkah    an Iban spear                                                       IBAN

kerengit    sandflies                                                          IBAN

engkabang    nut-like fruits of the *engkabang* tree, scientific name *Shorea* IBAN
     *macrophylla*, also known in English as illipe nuts

apong   hand-rolled palm leaf cigarette                                    IBAN

mupuk aku   "I'm leaving"                                                   IBAN

Pelagus   The Pelagus rapids along the upper Rajang River have claimed
     many lives. Local folklore connects the deadly rapids with a mythical
     giant serpent called Nabau. In some versions of the legend, Nabau
     took on human form to seduce the wife of a warrior in Pelagus. The
     warrior discovered what had happened and caught Nabau, cutting
     his body into seven pieces and throwing him into the rapids. Before
     Nabau died, he transformed back to his serpent form and uttered a
     curse that he would take his revenge on the locals. The seven rocks at
     the Pelagus rapids are said to be the seven pieces of Nabau's body.
     Locals still give offerings to appease Nabau, asking him not to claim
     lives at Pelagus.

Mayau and Angkabang   names of brothers from Nanga Anchau, Katibas;
     Angkabang is Kulleh Grasi's father.

Aki   grandfather                                                          IBAN

Aram   "come"                                                             IBAN

Bejalailah   "go, then, on your journey"                                    IBAN

tugal   a tool used to dig a hole in the earth to keep paddy seeds

Rejang   another version of Rajang, the great river of Sarawak and longest   IBAN
     river in Malaysia

Kebat   a garment made from *pua* cloth                                     IBAN

lampit   traditional engraved silver belt                                   IBAN

rawai   corset                                                            IBAN

Selampai Buri   a sack decorated with shells                               IBAN

Baju Taya   a vest worn during ceremonies                                  IBAN

buluk gerunong siong   a silver bell                                       IBAN

Apak   father                                                             IBAN

mulong   sago worm                                                         IBAN

Raja Sempulang Gana   a god from the Iban pantheon                         IBAN

Sendi Dara Anja   the name of an Iban girl                                 IBAN

Pua rayong   Iban ceremonial cloth                                        IBAN

Lang Jawang   singing eagle                                               IBAN

joget   a traditional Malay social dance                                  MALAY

Tali Kebayu   spirit medium                                              IBAN

Sendi   the name of an Iban girl                                          IBAN

kemenyan   benzoin resin, an aromatic resin used throughout the          MALAY
    Malay Archipelago as an incense, often associated with
    mystical attributes

langsat   a tropical fruit with translucent flesh and pale yellow-brown   MALAY
    skin, known as lanzones in English, scientific name *Lansium*
    *parasiticum*

Asai ke meda bali berinjan...   "observing the metamorphosis of an        IBAN
    incident"

bunsu   spirit                                                           IBAN

ketupung   one of the seven omen birds, scientific name *Sasia abnormis*  IBAN

ensera   story or legend                                                 IBAN

lalang   long wild grass                                                 MALAY

Niang Inik Bangan   the late grandmother, named Bangan

baik pua tok Jang...   "carry this cloth, young man, and walk among the   IBAN
    best"

Nya baru terkinsit pintu langit...   "the door of the sky opens, the three IBAN
    stars shine, promising to open pathways for the children on mankind"

sebayan   the afterworld                                                 IBAN

bunian   the invisible realm                                            MALAY

pua   The *pua kumbu* is an Iban ceremonial cloth woven by women.         IBAN
    The patterns on a *pua kumbu* represent mythological narratives,
    family geneologies, or personal stories.

pulai   return                                                          IBAN

manjong   war cry                                                       IBAN

Sangkuh   spear                                                         IBAN

ilang   sword                                                           IBAN

Pengayau   headhunter                                                   IBAN

ai jalong   drink of triumph

lekapadi   paddy seeds                                                  IBAN

**Ibun**   to guard or look after                                                                                IBAN

**Sengalang**   refers to Sengalang Burong, the warrior god, the most                 IBAN
powerful deity in the Iban pantheon

**Ketupung**   if this omen bird is heard during paddy harvest season, it is        IBAN
considered a bad omen

**Inik Andan Rabong Menua, Inik Indi Rabong Ari**   refers to Inik Andan, a        IBAN
sister of Sengalang Burong

**Sera Gunting**   One of the most important cultural figures in Iban                   IBAN
mythology, a demi-god, son of an ancient Iban hunter and Dara
Tinchin Temaga, the daughter of Sengalang Burong. Sengalang Burong
taught his grandson Sera Gunting the customary laws of the Iban
people, including rituals for farming, headhunting, and death.

**Endu Chempaka Tempurung Alang**   Sera Gunting's aunt, with whom Sera        IBAN
Gunting engaged in incest

**Dini alai nuan Seramugah...**   "Where are you, Seramugah, the one who        IBAN
guards the land, who knows the good and bad places for hill paddy?
Where are you Seragindi, the one who guards the water source of
unfathomable depths, the upstream of many rivers?"

**genselan**   offerings                                                                                   IBAN

**bejalai**   to wander, roam                                                                          IBAN

**Gerasi Nading Bujang Berani Kempang**   Gerasi Nading is a figure in Iban        IBAN
mythology who was expelled from the celestial realm of Panggau Libau
to live in the human realm. Gerasi Nading Bujang Berani Kempang is a
term of enderarment given to brave young warriors.

**Buluh Antu**   an Iban village in the area of Betong, Serawak

**Skrang**   a river in the area of Sri Aman, Sarawak

**tangsang kenyalang**   the abode of the hornbill                                               IBAN

**Ketupong, Beragai, Pangkas, Embuas, Kelabu Papau, Burung Malam,**        IBAN
**Bejampung**   the seven omen birds

**DON'T** 57

**ensurai**   a wild plant that grows by river banks in the rural areas of        IBAN
Sarawak, with red fruit-flowers with wings

**sireh**   betel leaf                                                                                     MALAY

**Aki**   grandfather                                                                                     IBAN

# CIRCUMFERENCE BOOKS

Circumference Books is a press for poetry in translation.
Our books highlight the process of translation and how that work is
rooted in collaboration. Each multi-lingual project foregrounds original
design solutions, making visual the relationships between languages,
cultures, writers, and translators. Circumference Books supports the creative
and urgent work of bridging cultures and languages. Our projects spotlight
non-national languages and foster cross-linguistic poetic exchange.

*Circumference Books would not be possible without our*

## FOUNDING MEMBERS

Carrie Olivia Adams · Mohan Ambikaipaker · Stephanie Anderson
Jeffrey Angles · Mary Jo Bang · Jessica Baran · Josephine Beeman
Charles Bernstein & Susan Bee · Paul Bisagni · Elaine Bleakney
Christine & Patrick Brosnan · Anthony Brosnan · Natalee Caple
Jennifer Chang · Don Mee Choi · Allyson Clay · Hillary Cookler
Roewan Crowe · Lizzie Davis · Mónica de la Torre · Sharon Dolin
Danielle Dutton · Timothy Farrington · Elaine Garza · Joseph Giardini
Gabrielle Giattino · Eric Giroux · Sonja Greckol · Sandra Guerreiro
Lucy Ives · Donna Kane · Esther Kim · Wonder Koch · Rita Kronovet
the Kronovet Cataño family · Brett Fletcher Lauer · Angie Lee
Paul Legault · Martha Lewin & Jack Egan · Eugene Lim · Eric Lundgren
Tamerra Moeller · Trey Moody · Erín Moure · Paul Myers · Idra Novey
Carl Phillips · Nicolas Rapold · Sally Rosenberg · Emily Schlink
James Shea & Dorothy Tse · Amy Shearn · David Shook · Molly Spencer
Christina Svendsen · Zach Tackett · Eddie Tejeda · Hugh Thomas
Eric Trozzo · Uncle Richie · Karen Van Dyck · Lawrence Venuti
Gerard Visel · Cathy Wagner · Michael Welt · Robert Whitehead
Jesse Wilbur · Jeffrey Yang · Rachel Zucker

Find out more about membership:

*www.circumferencebooks.com*